I REMEMBER

INDIANAPOLIS YOUTH WRITE ABOUT THEIR LIVES

MARTIN LUTHER KING COMMUNITY CENTER

2024

Edited by
Emily Mack

Copyright 2024
INWords Publications
Indiana Writers Center
All rights reserved
I Remember: Indianapolis Youth Write about Their Lives
ISBN: 978-1-7324993-2-4
INWords Publications, Indianapolis, IN
Printed in the United States of America

Indiana Writers Center
Building a Rainbow
Youth Public Memoir Project

Executive Director: Sarah Ginter
Writer in Residence: Barbara Shoup
Program Coordinator: Barbara Shoup
Instructors: Emily Mack and Celeste Williams

Thank You to Our Generous Funders

IndyStar.

Indianapolis Woman's Club

 | **National Endowment for the Arts**
arts.gov

Special thanks to Kate Shoup

Barbara Shoup

Writer-in-Residence, Indiana Writers Center
Building a Rainbow Coordinator
Instructor

The Indiana Writers Center's summer learning program, Building a Rainbow, served sixty students at the Martin Luther King Community Center during the summer of 2024, helping them their writing and literacy skills by writing about their own lives. The program is named after a colorful, whimsical poster of a half-made rainbow that is covered with tiny stick figures painting, hammering and operating cranes as they work to finish it. The image is a visual reminder that there are many small steps in creating something beautiful—a piece of writing, a dream a goal, a life.

Working one-on-one, IWC instructors and volunteers helped the MLK writers to turn their memories into words and encouraged them to reflect upon their experiences. Sharing their writing with one another during "Authors Chair" taught them to believe that their voices matter.

I love to sit down with young writers and help them tease out a memory by asking questions. What's the first thing that happened? What happened next. And next. Where were you? Who else was there? What were you wearing? What did you *do*? Say? What did others do or say? How did you feel? How did you show that feeling? If you didn't show the feeling, what was it like kept inside you—a fire, a dull pain in your heart, a rocket about to burst into the air?

Sometimes students heave a sigh of boredom when the questions begin, but eventually they start answering, almost in spite of themselves. Pretty soon, they sit up a little straighter, lean forward—and then, best of all, they start to smile—and I know a story has come alive inside them.

At this point, they often say something that would make a good first sentence.

"Write that down," I say. "And keep going."

They do. And, as if by magic, the story begins to unspool. I leave them, bent over the page, writing furiously, and move on, hungry for that moment of combustion with another student. And then another.

This is happening all over the room. The air is full of stories the world needs to hear.

So we collected them and put them in this book.

It was a pleasure and a privilege to work with the MLK young writers this summer.

Enjoy their vibrant voices!

Monique Love

Martin Luther King Community Center
Literacy Program Director

The Martin Luther King Center Indy (The MLK Center) Summer Literacy Camp consisted of teaching literacy strategies and writing techniques for all students who participated in the camp. The role of the MLK Center Summer Literacy Camp was to provide students with continuous learning and expectations. Daily, the students participated in improving their reading and comprehension skills and their creative writing.

Alongside the MLK Center, the Indiana Writing Center created an 8-week writing workshop that focused the students on constructing an anthology of their writing over a series of topics ranging from challenges to successes and from humor to gravity. The students' approach to writing opened and further exposed them to the idea of "getting their thoughts down on paper."

This book shares the significant experiences of each student from kindergarten to 8th grade, and sheds light on their unique perspectives of the world.

Thank you for reading and engaging with the students through this book.

Emily Mack

Head Instructor
Anthology Editor

The first promise we make every summer to our young writers is, "This isn't like school writing." We tell them, "We are your editors." Inevitably, some of them, especially the older kids who have many years of "school writing" behind them, don't know what to make of that. They ask for help with spelling. They may wonder if they're doing it "right". They may hesitate to begin at all, instead filling the margins of their page with doodles or shrinking into their beloved hoodie. And so, we come alongside them and ask, "What do you think? What do you remember? What do you see? What did you do next?" And the words begin to flow.

I am a teacher. I spend 180 days a year making literacy accessible for hundreds of disabled and neurodiverse teenagers as a special education teacher. Of course I think phonics, spelling, and grammar are important. Of course I want to encourage logical thought and precise word choice and many other skills. But when we begin to see writing as just a list of skills to be mastered, we lose the wonder. This summer—for me and for our children—was a breath of fresh air. We were allowed—encouraged—to be creative. To play. To draw with bright colors. To express opinions on everything from neighborhood violence to the newest Disney movie. To share memories of the people and places close to us.

The young people we got to write with this summer are artists and athletes. They are brothers and sisters and cousins. They are creative and insightful. Honest and kind. Funny and intelligent. I've been blessed to participate in this program for eight years now. I am drawn back year after year by the concentration in kids' faces as they hunch over their notebooks, and by the confidence in their stance as they read their work aloud for the first time.

In our final week together, I asked the kids to share their hopes and goals for the new school year. "I hope I have a nice teacher. I want to get better at football. I want to become a better reader. I hope my mom lets me try gymnastics classes. I hope I make new friends."

Let me share my own hopes for them:

- I hope they remember their unique stories deserve to be heard.
- I hope they continue to be proud of their words and share them loudly.
- I hope they continue to write (even when they don't "have to").

It is pure joy to write with Indianapolis' young people every summer, and it is an honor to be trusted with their stories. I hope you enjoy them as much as I do.

Celeste Williams

Indiana Writers Center Board Member
Instructor

It is the hundredth anniversary of the birth of one of my literary heroes, James Baldwin. In 1962, a letter he wrote to his namesake, James, his brother's son, was published. The letter is as much a note of love to his nephew, as it is a warning about the racism that will surely touch the young Black man's life... "to strengthen you against the loveless world. ...."

He said, ".... am writing this letter to you to try to tell you something about how to handle them, for most of them do not yet really know that you exist. ..."

Every time I have volunteered in this program to help children write about their lives, I want them to let people know they do exist, and they have very important things to say. As these young people become accustomed to us — not so much as teachers, but as facilitators — and realize we will not tell them they are wrong or can't spell or put a comma in the "wrong" place, they open up in wondrous ways.

Far from telling them to "sit down and shut up," we exhort them to write whatever comes to mind, and then to read their words "loud and proud."

Baldwin told his nephew: "...Take no one's word for anything, including mine, but trust your experience. Know whence you came. If you know whence you came, there is really no limit to where you can go."

I wrote the following poem in honor of our children and their voices. There is no limit to where they can go.

The Heads of Our Children

Dive beneath
the puffs, fades, ribbons, beads, dreds, curls, braids, twists,
kinks —
find entire worlds;
worlds that shine bright
as diamonds;
worlds as vast and as infinite
as the universe
as small and powerful
as the tiniest atom.
Ask them to let you in
and
they
hesitate —
because they have been told to
sit down
and
shut up
you are
wrong
you are
a failure
you don't

belong here
you don't
belong there.
They hide their heads
to protect their inner light
and
reach
toward the
seductive
glow
of screens —
which give them
everything
but
love.
Listen to them,
really
listen.
They have so much
to say.
Don't be surprised.
Their voices
were
always
there.

Table of Contents

Kindergarten and First-Grade Writers 1
    Aiden.. 2
    Alonna.. 3
    Baylee.. 5
    Bella... 6
    Dante.. 8
    Divine... 9
    Jayce 10
    Kaden 11
    Kali.. 13
    Kyree 15
    Monte.. 17
    Nalani.. 18
    Sa'Riyah 19
    Somayah... 20
    Te'lia 21
    Terrell.. 23
Second- and Third-Grade Writers 25
    Addison... 26

A'Layah 28

Ameelia 30

Ayden 31

DeMel 33

DeShawn 34

Devaughn 35

Edan 36

Eli 37

Iyanna 38

JaNiyla 39

Kyrah 40

Layla 42

Mahiya 43

Nyla 45

Riylee 47

Synila 48

Fourth- and Fifth-Grade Writers 51

Darrell 52

DJ 55

D'Laynah 57

Kahayra 58

KeyShawn 59

Kobe	60
Leah	61
Naylyn	62
Tommie	64
Middle-School Writers	65
Atlanta	66
Austin	67
Eric	69
Gabriel (Middle School Teacher)	71
Isaac	73
Jai'Anna	75
James	76
Jordyn	77
Kathy	78
Nikkal	80
Phillip	82
Sirion	84
Syncere	85
Writing Prompts	89

Kindergarten and First-Grade Writers

Aiden

The Park

When I was at the park, I was running and I tripped and fell and hurt my leg. When I got in the car, my mama took me to the store to get some swords.

Creepy Clowns

When I fell asleep I was scared in the dark. I was afraid. I was trying to fight the creepy clown. I punched the clowns and said, "I will punch you! Get away from me creepy clowns!"

Trampoline

When I was jumping on the trampoline, I hurt myself and I walked into the house to try and tell my mom.

Alonna

Tea Party

I have a Gabby Dream House and I love to play with it! It has 5 floors. It has decorations like heart lights on the walls. It's special to me. The kitchen got a picture of Gabby and a picture of a cat. Her room is pink. her room has a picture of her and she has a doll.

I have a toy stuffy. It's a white teddy bear. My big sister and I play tea party with it. I have a pink table for the tea party. I have fake tea in my tea pot. My teapot has flowers and hearts around it. I make real tea for me, my sister, and my friend Kali, and fake tea for my bear and my dolls. We eat fake cake. We dress up in fancy dresses. I have a fancy hat with pink and purple flowers and hearts. I roast marshmallows at my tea party, and I put sugar in my tea. We have strawberries, too.

I Am From

I am from Indiana
Coco the cat
My purple and black braids
My sparkly clothes
Macaroni and cheese
I go to journey to eat crab legs.
I crack them open. Yum!
I like to have fun and I like to run.
Love, Alonna

My Community

My family is a community. My mom and my dad and my brothers. I am the only girl. I like being the only girl because I have my own room. I live in a doubled house. My favorite part of my community is to go to the pool.

Camping

When I was 2 years old I went camping in the backyard with my big sister and I got scared of the dark. I heard crawling sounds and my big sister took me back in the house and I slept in the house. I went camping when I was older and I'm not scared anymore.

Baylee

Barbies

I play Barbie with my sister at my mom's house. We play together. We each have a Barbie. We make them swim. We put their swimsuits on. We are in a big pool. Me and my cousin go to my cousin's house. It's a little bit far. Her mom cooks cool stuff. She cooks chicken. She lets us eat cake and snacks. She makes some fries.

My Cousin

I love my cousin Brooklyn. She was playing with me in the water with water balloons. We were having fun with each other. We talked to each other, we eat chicken together. She's older than me. She's seventeen. She has braids and beads in her hair. She cooks at church. Sometimes we have a sleepover at my house. We play with Barbie dolls.

My Best Day

I have fun with my cousins and my besties. We had a sleepover. We played with Barbies. We went to the park. We went to Disneyland and met Mickey Mouse. Me and Bella played with sand. We read princess books together. The best part about having a twin is playing princesses together. We play unicorns together. We went on a field trip to the zoo together. I saw a horse. She saw a pig.

Bella

My Dragon

It was a big swimming pool. The water was blue. Me and my sister and my mom were there. My mom taught me to swim. I was scared at first. My mom held me up. She let me go and I started swimming.

My large dragon is blue and she has a little pink hair and big blue hair. Soft hair. You press a button and she lights up. She eats whatever I give her. She eats cold fish and swims in the water. I found her in the sea. She's kind of real. She eats cooked fish, too. She has blue, purple and pink lines in her hair. She gives me hugs when I go to MLK and give me a piece of sour-sweet candy. If she's hungry, I take her outside to get some food. She flies. She follows me wherever I go.

I love dragons. I found a blue one in the water. She is real. She gives me hugs when I go to MLK. She eats fish. Her name is Seesue. She eats seafish and she loves to take names with me. My mom tells me to go to bed and Seesue wakes me up. She wants to me to go find some grass in the sea but there's no grass in the sea.

My Baby Sister

I am feeling happy because my baby sister came over. We went to the park and I pushed her on the swings. She smiled and laughed which made me happy. We went to the fair and we went on the roller coaster. I held my little sister. It was slow for the baby but it had lots of zig zags. When she was trying to get a cookie she fell down but she was brave. We went to the doctor to check my little sister out.

My Name

My nickname is Panda. My mama calls me Brittany because it's my second middle name. My sister has the same middle name. My mom calls me panda because I'm cute like a panda bear.

Dante

Learning to Ride a Bike

The first time I rode a bike without training wheels was excited because I stayed on the bike while I pedaled. I did it all by myself.

I Love

I love swimming.
I love cake.
I love football – catching and throwing.
I love spaghetti.
I love Applebees.
I don't like Fruity Pebbles.

My Favorite Places

Beach with my family
Flag football with my friend from school
Movies, Inside Out 2
Home

Divine

My Name

My name is Divine but Divvy is my nickname. My mama calls me Divvy. My brother calls me Devon, but I don't like it because it's a boy name.

Love Mommy. I love My Dad.

I love my baby brother.

Starbucks

My favorite place to go is Starbucks. I get a strawberry cake pop. I go with my mommy. And I get a coffee. It's hot with whipped cream on top. I got apples and boiled eggs and craisins.

Jayce

I Love

I love my dog Harley.
Fireworks.
I love the pool. I jump in.
Vanilla ice cream.
Play tag. "you're IT!"
I love going to the trampoline park.

Trampoline Park

The first time I went to the trampoline park I went with my sister and my nephews and niece. I was excited because I can jump and do backflips. I learned to do backflips in my mom's room. It was easier to do backflips at the trampoline park. I was on the trampoline and I broke my leg! I didn't have to go to the hospital because I only broke it a little bit. It hurt for a while then it got better and I was jumping again. I really liked it and I've gone back to jump!

Swimming

When I was outside the pool, I sprinkled the water on my face, then my older sister dragged me in and threw me in the deep end. It was really hard to swim where I couldn't touch. I was crying! I hung onto the side and then I got out.

Kaden

The Mouse

My mommie saw a big mouse in the front room. My sister picked up the mouse trap and put cheese in the mouse trap. The mouse went for the cheese and got smushed. Then me and my sister were laughing. My mom was happy that the mouse was gone.

My Favorite Place

I go to my TiTi's house with my sister.

Birthday Party

My cousin went to a birthday party. He had fun. So did I. I went to gymnastics for my birthday and my big cousin jumped on the trampoline. I gave him a hug. I learned how to do a backflip.

My Sister

I love my little sister, Assir. She is a baby. She is not born yet, but it's okay. When she is born I am going to buy her a teddy bear and a Barbie doll to keep her happy.

My Best Day

I went to the water park and to McDonald's.

Movies

I went to the movies for my mom's birthday. I watched Inside Out 2. My sister Kyree came too. The movie had a dump of memories. Kyree was drinking her drink but then she felt a little teardrop on her face because of the memory when she was a baby. I had fruit candy and chocolate bars and sour patch.

Kali

My Toys

I see a play phone. And there is a fake purse. It is like a toy. There are two fake credit cards in the purse. I play with them in the park at School 43. I play with them at home, too. I call my best friend on my play phone. Her name is Alanna. We talk about Barbies and hair and dresses and shoes on the phone. I buy a Barbie Dream House with my credit cards. I want a Gabbie Doll House because it's big and it has hearts in it, in the bedroom, the kitchen, and the bathroom and living room. The hearts are cut in half and then come together on the door and windows. There is also a pool. Barbie likes the pool. She wears a pink and blue and purple one piece. Her daughter is in the pool, too. She has purple hair.

The Zoo

The first time I went to the zoo I was 5 years old. I saw a lion. It jumped at me and I got scared. I loved the monkeys. They were so cute. I wanted to keep them as my pet. I saw all the animals.

I Am From

I am from Indiana.
I love my friends. Nice.
I have a large family — seven brothers. I'm the princess in the family.
I have two dogs: one named Champ and one named Cocoa. Champ is a big dog and he plays with Cocoa. Cocoa is small and she's friendly.
My favorite food is crab legs. I don't like junk food.
I practice basketball with my brothers. I'm not really good. I can't make the shots. I'm still practicing.
My brothers are nice. They love me.
My mom and my newborn brother love me too.
On Father's Day I gave my dad a picture of me and him with hearts around it. And I wrote "love Kali" on it.

Kyree

My Barbie Doll House

My Barbie doll house is in my backyard near my pool. My Barbie doll house has a pool, too, that is square. It has six rooms and a working elevator. I play with the dollhouse with my sister. My doll house smells sweet, like candy canes, and it is pink and white. I like playing with my Barbie doll house.

My Baby Brother

I love my baby brother Asi. He's adorable! He smiles at me. He likes when I play with him. He likes balls because he throws them and rolls them.

I love when he comes in the front room and plays with us.

He's learning how to walk! He is so close. He knows how to walk but he don't. He keeps falling down on purpose because he knows how to crawl.

Day with Grandma

When I woke up at my grandma's house, we went to the park and McDonald's. She's my favorite because she takes us places that are fun to explore.

Peace Park

Peace means quiet where I swing on the swings.

Happiness

I feel happy because it's fun here. Writing a story and swimming are fun. And we go to the park. I do the monkey bars. My hands have bumps. I love doing them. I climb on top of them and slide down. Then I jump down. We have to learn and have fun at the same time. I like dressing up. My sister is a fashionista. So am I.

Monte

Laughing

I laugh really hard when my mommy tickles me. She wiggles her fingers in my middle. I like to laugh.

My Favorite Place

My favorite place to go is the park. I like to swing on the swings. I go really high. I go with my mama, and my brother and sister. I can spin on the swings. We go on the slide. I see basketball hoops and footballs and the spring around things.

Movies

The first time I went to the movies to see Inside Out 2. We got popcorn and a slushie. The lights went out and the movie started. I loved the orange man and the green woman.

Nalani

Kitty Cat Game

I love to play with my sister Nyla. We play an animal game on our tablets. We have to change the cats' colors. I be making them brown, black, and pink. I'm a baby cat, but I be growing. Meow!

My Goals

Hi, I'm Nyla's sister and she's helping me. Anyways, I want to be a cheerleader. I wish to be a teenager. I hope I will have a nice teacher. I think I will learn how to read and spell. Bye!

Firsts

Things I remember doing for the first time:
played with my brother
played on my tablet
ate sushi and crab legs
went to the zoo
first day of school

The first time I ate crab legs, I went to the sushi place and ate sushi. They were big and red. They tasted like crab legs!

Sa'Riyah

I Love

I love pizza and Barbies. I do my homework.

My Community

My community is a store with lots of toys.

Somayah

I Like

I like playing hide and seek.
I like eating pancakes.
I like drinking apple juice.
I like pancakes with strawberry syrup. My favorite is rainbow. I love food!

My Best Day

I went to the park. My favorite part is going down the slide with my sister and my brother.

Te'lia

The Sea

I love seafood. Juicy crab. I love finding crabs deep in the ocean. I was in the sea where I found a shark and he took me deep in the sea with his friends.

Weekend

I feel good today because over the weekend I went to the movie theater with my best friend Kali. I was getting ready to pass out because it was so hot so we went to the pool. The water cooled me off.

Best Day Ever

On the best day ever, I would want to go to Inside Out 2 and eat popcorn. I would go with Kali, Alonna, Bella, and Baylee.

My Name & My Favorite Place

I like my name. My nickname is Summer. I like going to the pool and the pool is my fav.

Lost

I got lost inside of the fair. Me and my auntie was walking behind my mom. We were getting ready to go. I kept looking down and when I looked up I couldn't see them. Some people found me. They asked me what was my momma's number and first I forgot, but then I remembered and they called her. When she found me she was crying.

Terrell

The Beach

I played at the beach. I played with friends. Their names were Bear and Darrel. My dog's name is Jimmy. He is a Golden Retriever.

I Love

I love swimming.
I love watching TV.
I love playing games.
I love crab legs and ribs.
I love octopus.
I love sweet potatoes.

My Name

My nickname is junior. My dad's name is Willy. I like my nickname.

My Favorite Place

My favorite place to go is home. Relaxing. I watch TV.

Basketball

The first time I made a basket. I made it on the first try! It made me feel so good!

Best Day Ever

On the best day ever, I would go to the movies to see Inside Out 2. I would eat spaghetti. My mom makes really yummy spaghetti because she is the best cook ever. I would go swimming with my sister Ameelia and my friend Te'lia. We would go to the zoo to see alligators.

Second- and Third-Grade Writers

Addison

My Teddy Bear

I had a big pink teddy bear. Her name was Maggie. She was fluffy. She said hello to me. I couldn't bring her outside so I played with her in my room. We played slime and play dough. I slept with her every day. Then we were at my grandma's house. My mom put her in the basement and we went to another house. But when we went back she wasn't there. There was a flood and she got nasty, smelly and my grandma had to throw her away. But she said she'd get me another.

Ode to My Bear

This is an ode to my teddy bear. She's brown with blue eyes. She's soft. She stays in my bed all day. We play Uno together. We watch scary movies together.

I Like

I like to ride my bike.
I like spaghetti.
I like Nina
I like Aqua, my cat.
I like to read.
I like to draw.
I like to play.
I like to climb.

My Community

I only got 1 brother
I love my family
I love my dad
I love my mom
I love my sister
I love my brother

A'Layah

My Teddy Bear

I had a big brown teddy bear when I was seven. It was about my size. Its name was Strawberry Cup. My Papa gave it to me. I played in my room with it and acted like it was a friend. I said, "Hi, Teddy tear." I made him say, "Hello." And I love her. She loves me. She's my best friend.

I Like

I like hair bows
and my clothes
My friends
My mom
My nini
I like Roblox

My Community

I love my community because I can play with my dog. And I like to go to the carnival.

Wishes For Next School Year

I want to read.
I wish I can do gymnastics.
I hope I will be good at it.
I think I will learn Spanish.

A'Lariah
I am Alayiah

Ameelia

Ode to Piano

I like the sounds.
I love the fun sounds.
I feel excited when my fingers make music.
It feels like you're touching buttons.
The black keys sound low
the white keys sound higher.
It's like reading, but it tells you
how to press the keys.
When I play it makes me feel so excited.
Music sounds fun to my ears.
I play Godzilla for my brother.
He says, "Whoa! I didn't know you could do that!"
I learn by myself.
I teach myself. I don't have a piano.
I learn on my phone.
When I grow up I'm going to have a house and put a piano in it.

I Like

I like to play piano and listen to music.
I like all songs.
I am from my mom and my brother Terrell.
I am from Meridian.
I like to ride my skateboard.
I like to play with my friends.
We play Twister and gymnastics
laugh and play, tickle each other.

Ayden

My Name

My nickname is Allen. My mom gave me the name. I really like my nickname. Nobody else calls me by my nickname. Only my mom. I like my name. It's cool! My dad's name is Jonathan. Allen is my middle name.

My Community

The children's museum is part of my community. The movie theater is where I like to go. I like the restaurants in my community. Panda Express is my favorite.

I Am From

Football
Riding my bike in the driveway
Playing with my friends
Hot dogs
Mac and cheese
I have 3 sisters
It makes me sad to be the only boy because I don't have any brothers
I like to go to the park
I love to go on the swings and make new friends

Funny!

My sister makes me laugh!
My cousin makes me laugh!
We were playing hide and seek. I fell in the grass. It was super funny. I had grass stains on my jeans. My mom said it was OK. I felt good.

DeMel

Laughter

I was in the cafeteria and I was trying not to laugh at my friend, but I laughed so hard that snot came out of my nose. It was so funny. I don't get embarrassed when I laugh.

Rollercoaster

There was a time I was brave when on a roller coaster with a loopy-loop. I am scared of heights but I went anyway. When I got off, my mom made a funny face, and it made me laugh. So I was brave and funny, too.

My Favorite Things

This is a picture of my shelf with my favorite things. The rock, blanket, teddy bear Piddle, Rocky, Mr. Blankie, and She Rainbow. I love all these things because they're cute.

DeShawn

Laughter

I love to make people laugh. At my birthday party I drank water then somebody said something funny. Then the water came out of my nose because I was laughing so hard!!! Everybody laughed!!!

Christmas

On Christmas, I said I want a pair of crocs. I woke up on Christmas morning and there was a shoebox. I hoped it was Cheerio crocs. But there was coal on top. I had to dig under the coal to find my Nintendo switch. Then my mom said, "There's something else in there." And there was! There was an Amazon firestick under the switch. Then I got a bunch of toys. I got everything I wanted. I was so happy!

My Community

At a park, I had a family reunion. My TT took me to the party. We have water balloon fights and lots of fun. I saw relatives I hadn't seen in a long time. It made me happy.

Goals for The New School Year

I want to run track and learn to read better.

Devaughn

My Name

Hi my name is Devaughn. I'm a jr. Do I like being a jr? No. Because every time someone see me they be like wassup jr. I be like don't call me that.

Edan

Backflips

Something funny I did was a backflip. My brother was there and we laughed. He said it was cool and I did it outside. I think it was brave that I did it outside. Before the backflip, I was swimming. My family also taught me to swim. I got to play tag with other kids at the pool. It was fun. I ate Cheetos while at the pool as well.

Blueberries

I thought about blueberries. They are round and purple and they taste good. They turn my tongue purple!

My Name

My mom made my name. I like my name. My friends call me Edan Lumpkins. And my brother call me peanut. And I call my brother Big Bugey.

Community

I love my community! My family is in my community. My favorite part of my community is the park. I like the swings.

Eli

I Am From

1. Football
2. Basketball
3. I help in the kitchen
4. Cool
5. Slow
6. Gets up early
7. Dreds

My Nickname

My nickname is Boogie. My mom name me. My mom call me by my nickname.

My Community

My perfect community would have basketball courts and football fields. People would be helpful. I would play with my friends.

A Picture

I see a picture of me in shorts. My mom took the picture. I look happy. I was at home. Summer. Red shorts. Smiling.

Iyanna

I Am From

I am from seafood.
My dog's name is Bella.
My favorite music is I just got back with my ex.
My favorite dance is I just got back with my ex.
My favorite place is Urban Air.
My nickname is unique.

JaNiyla

Fourth of July

That day on the fourth of July at my titi's house a firework bounce on the car and went everywhere. All of kids ran into the house. But the parents stayed outside.

Community

I like the park
And I love the square.
I love hanging out with me and Engelin and her sisters and friends.

Kyrah

Walking

Sometimes me and my siblings walk to the park. It takes 5 minutes to get there. We pass a McDonald's and a gas station. Sometimes we stop for ice cream or Reeses. Sometimes I get a slushee. I mix sour and sweet flavors. At the park I love to swing and climb on the ropes. My brother goes and plays basketball. My sister goes to the playground.

I Am From

I am from Indy. I am from 36th street.
I am from cake.
I am from pools.
I am from Nala.
I am from drawing.
I am from McDonald's happy meals. "McDoodles" is what I say.
I am from Phillip my brother.
I am from Sariah my sister.
I am the youngest.
K.K. is my nickname.

My Name

My mom named me after her childhood friend. My middle name is Melissa. That's my grandma, my dad's mom. When we were younger my grandma would let us have sleepovers at her house. There were only two rooms so I would sleep in my grandma's room. She had a little pink bed for me on the floor next to her bed. I feel good about being named after my grandma.

Barbeque

Sometimes me and my siblings walk to the gas station and there are people gathering inside. They're making a barbecue inside the gas station. Sometimes they give us some of what they're barbequing like hot dogs or something on a stick. For free! Sometimes they ask us to go get barbeque sauce from McDonalds. When I see them I feel good.

Layla

I Am From

I am from a house with a red door and a back door that's white.

I Like

1. Cheerleading
2. Football
3. Seafood
4. Flips
5. Helping my mom
6. The Moon Girl and the Devil Dragon
7. Bracelets
8. Nails
9. Graceland Ave
10. I have a dog named Harley.

Mahiya

Roller Coasters

I went on a roller coaster with my mom and it went around and around and around. And we hanged upside down for a second. It was scary! My mom said she was going to close her eyes and then she opened eyes back up and it was still going and going. I had a ponytail in my hair and it went flying. I was brave. Everybody was screaming. My mom said there was no buckle but there was a bar that came down. My mom didn't really want to go but I made her go with me.

Ode to My Family

An ode to my family. My mom and dad and dog.
I love to bake sweet cake pops and watch cake videos.
An ode to my dad.
My dad is fun. I watch movies with my dad.

Cake Pops

My mom and I used to make cake pops with sprinkles. I would make a dough ball, put a stick in it, dip it in white frosting, and then put pink and heart sprinkles and rainbow sprinkles and many other kinds. Then I would let them sit for a second. They tasted so sweet. I ate four. It was too good!

Holiday World

I went to Holiday World two weeks ago with my mom, dad, and big cousin. I went to the water park first because I wanted Dippin Dots. Then we went to the big water park. There were 4 or 5 slides, and I went on all of them but the last one. The line was SOOOOO long so I just didn't want to go on that one. The best part was getting to swim. I wanted to go to the lazy river, but my mom and big cousin said I had to wear a floatie.

Nyla

Bravery

When I was at the park I wanted to jump off this really high rock climbing thing, but it was too high. So I started to get scared but I noticed a little voice in my head said, "Don't be scared, Nyla. You won't fall. Remember, be brave. Breathe in and out." So I did what the little voice said and then, "Wee!" I go off. And that's the story of me being brave. Remember, always be brave.

My Bear

I had a blue teddy bear that looked like a dragon. I got it for Christmas. It was my favorite. I had it when I was seven. I loved it. Here is a picture of it!

What I Like To Do

Things I like to do is do my hair and go shopping, eat, sleep, and play with my siblings. I love to play with them but they're annoying. Anyways, my favorite toy is….actually I don't have a favorite. They're all ugly…I am from Indianapolis and I like this place called yummy bowl.

My Name

Hello guys! Lemme tell you about my name. I'm named after my gg her name is LaShauna Marie Daniel and mine is Nyla Marie Churchwell. We have the same middle name! When I was born my mom would tell them "it's Nyla, not Nala". So my gg has the same middle name as me. My dad's name is Daris Churchwell. Anyway bye! 🖤 Wait! and my nickname is Ny Ny. Now bye! 🖤

Riylee

Football

I like football.
I like it when they throw the ball.
I like it when I catch the ball.
I like playing football.
Football is my dream game.
I like catching the ball with 1 hand.
I love football and watching movies.
I like music.
I'm from Chicago.
My nickname is King.

Synila

Ode to Cheerleading

This is an ode to my cheer team. I love my team so much. I treat them like my sisters. We dance so hard my coaches almost cried. We spend so much time with each other like we're sisters. My coaches are the best coaches I can ask for.

I Am From

My dog Lyliah.
My cats china and princess.
Sushi.
Music like sza. My favorite song is saturn.
I am from Dance and Holland Michigan
I am from my hair.
I am from my mom and my dad. I am from my bed and my little brother.

Dollar Tree

I never thought they would shut down dollar tree, but they is!
They is!
They shutting down dollar tree. They is! They is!
I love dollar tree.
I thought it will be there forever.

My Name

My nickname is Baby D. I got my nickname off of a movie it's called ohh wait I forgot silly me. PLS don't call me that. All my siblings on my mom's side: Synija, Syncere, Synila, SynTrell. Baby D out.

Fourth- and Fifth-Grade Writers

Darrell

My Name

My dad name me. Ima jr. I love my name. My name is very rare and my nickname is DJ. DJ is for Darrell Boozer Jr. I don't got a middle name it's ok for me because I don't want one. but thank you for reading. Bye bye bye!!

My Community

My community is a lot of people and a lot of toys for kids. There would be toy cars and dirt bikes for kids to drive. There would be soccer fields. Everything would be free. There would be no kidnapping, no violence, no killing. There would be lots of pink trees. No bad people in my community.

Dirt Bike

I was four when I got my first dirt bike. It was a grey and black and gassed up bike. I still got it, but it's rusty. When I was 8, I got in a crash with it. I was riding on the strip and I looked back but I was still going. I crashed into a car as it was leaving. I hit my head and it was bleeding. My friends got off of their bikes and ran to help me. They rolled my dirt bike into the driveway. My dad took me to the hospital. I still got the scar but I got a new dirt bike. It was like my old one, but bigger and faster.

An Ode to My Family

We love to go to Chicago.
We love to go to the beach and I can see through the water
and see all the little fish!
We go to the movie theater then go home and watch another
movie.

Fourth Of July

Hi my name is Darrell. I love the 4th of July. I like fireworks. We go downtown for the fireworks. It's fun. The fireworks start little then they get big. It covers the whole downtown. My favorite kind of firework is called the devil cat. It's huge. My dad's brother gets his fireworks from Chicago. My mom and dad will let me do it and I will laugh. So that's what I do! Bye bye!!

DJ

Memories

When I was little my mom made mac and cheese and I used to watch Sponge Bob. I used to come home from school. She used to ask me how was school and I would say good. I'd sit in the living room and watch TV. When I was done eating I'd play outside. I'd ride my bike and play basketball with the neighbors. They used to beat me sometimes but that encourage me to try harder.

My Dog

I love my dog because it is basically family. My dog's name is Calvin. 6 yo in human years. 36 in dog years. When I play basketball he runs and tries to guard me. He is a golden retriever.

Fourth of July

On the fourth of July we are barbequing and our cousins and friends too. All of the adults help cook: my uncles, my mom, my papa. We make burgers and hot dogs. The kids play on the trampoline and play football. I have a lot of cousins. Most of them are younger than me. Sometimes we play kickball and everybody plays. For other holidays, like graduations, we'll see who knows the person best. Everyone brings fireworks! We probably have over 100. we go to my grandma's house. Her house is huge. The fireworks look like a red flare.

My Name

My mom named me Derric Allan Burrus and my nickname DJ for Derric Jr. If I will change my name it would be Mike. I like being a jr so people will know I'm somebody's kid.

D'Laynah

Ode to My Cheer Team

I love how they respect me and how we have fun together and hype each other up and spend time together.

I Am From

I'm from Indiana.
And I love to do hair and I like Tiktok.
I like taking naps and eating.
I run track and do cheer and dance.
I can do backflips off the trampoline.

My Name

My mama call me Yavia. I don't like it cause it's weird. My sisters call me Laynah and my dad call me twin. My mom name me by idk and I would change my name to DayDay.

Pride

I'm proud of myself because I made the track team and the cheerleading team. And getting through 5th grade and trying my best through 5th. It was hard to try to get through 5th grade but I did it. Oh, and I'm proud of myself because I did somebody hair and I did good.

Kahayra

My Sister

In my imagination, I see my sister. She is older, happy. She is wearing a Nike shirt and Nike pants without shoes. I haven't seen her in a long time. She is 13. Her name is Kianah. I think I'm going to see her today. She's nice. We grew up together. I miss her a lot.

KeyShawn

My Pets

I love my cat because I like to play with him. Toy mice and soccer. When he pushes a toy with his paws. He liked to play hide and seek, too. He would meow when he wanted to eat. He was a garden cat. He watched the garden.

I like to play with my dog. I like to play tug of war with her. Her name is Lana. She's a poodle. We also have a Frenchie puppy named King.

Kobe

My Name

I wasn't named after Kobe Bryant, but I like him. My dad named me. My mom wanted to name me Gerald Jr. My dad and brother are both named Gerald.

Fourth of July

On the 4th of July it was a Sunday. I went to the store and I went to get some snacks and some chicken and some ribs to BBQ and went to the fireworks store. When I got back home I went to my room to play 2K and my mom said it's time to cook some chicken and some ribs.

Leah

Ode to Ginger

This is an ode to my puppy Ginger who is so cute when she's playing with her toys. I like to take her for a walk to my friend's house. I feed her food and give her water. She wiggles her tail. She likes to take naps.

I Am From

Braids with beads. My favorite is pink and purple.
I like to ride my bike at my dad's house.
Pizza is my favorite food.
Playing with Ginger, my puppy.
I ask a lot of questions.

What Makes Me Proud of Myself

I make my own food. I make my bed every day, and I make art, and I keep my room clean.

Goals for Next School Year

I want to get better at reading, spelling, and math. I want to play basketball.

Naylyn

Burns

I was playing with my Elmo toy while my mom was cooking spaghetti. And I touched the stove and on my hand it felt like somebody set my hand on fire. We went to Riley Children's Hospital. I rode in a wagon a red one. They put me in a room filled with stickers.

What I Love

I love walking the trail/it helps me calm down and BURN off steam with sound, my dog/when I'm not in the mood he comes and plays with me/gino my mom/even tho she ignoring my granny/ I miss you my friends/they're always there for me when I need them

My Community

In my perfect community peace more love nonviolence more chick-fil-a in a city. Sunny every day. Everybody can have more than one day of their birthday.

My Talents

I am proud of myself because I made the track team and I can cook.

Cooking: Me and my sisters made lobster, steak, and boiled eggs. I get my cooking skills from my grandparents. They are both chefs at "The Living Room Lounge"

Track: I love running, but I quit track because the coach was annoying and kept making me mad. So I quit but I ended up going back somehow.

Tommie

My Friends

My friends make me laugh. They tell funny jokes and put on funny videos and they play with me when we play basketball. I try to jump but I can't. When they dunk, I try to dunk but I can't. It inspired me to try harder to dunk. And then one day I finally got it. It felt good.

My Motorcycle

When I was 3 or 4 or 5 I had a motorcycle with a battery. I rode outside at my dad's apartment. It was tannish blue. I had a Paw Patrol car. I drove it in the house and outside. I felt like I was really driving. I had a skateboard and a hoverboard. No wheels, no play. When I grow up, I want to have a Hellcat. That's a fast car.

Ouch!

Since you asked, I"ll tell you why I'm feeling mad! Because I stepped on a nail–twice! It happened because I was running in slides at my friend's house. There was a nail in the yard. the first time I thought there was something in my shoe, but there wasn't. When I took my shoe off there was a dent in my foot! I thought nothing of it, but then I put my shoe back on and it pushed into my foot. It hurt! I grabbed my foot. My friends walked me home and I was hopping on one foot. Now I listen to my mom when she says,"Wear shoes when you go play."

Middle-School Writers

Atlanta

Ode to Food

This is an ode to food. It helps me survive so I can stay alive.
There are so many to choose from
They are all around the world. You can never go wrong with food. There's different types of foods from different places. There's Mexican, Chinese and much more to eat. It's very very good.
That's why I love to eat!

My Name

My parents named me Atlanta. I don't know why they decided to name me after a city but it's unique. If I could change my name I would change it to Nicole because Nicole is my middle name and I don't know what other name to choose.

Pride

Something that makes me proud of myself is when I speak in public and when I speak loud because I have a soft voice. Something else that makes me proud of myself is when I figure out how to do something by myself because I normally need help with a lot of things. Here is a time when I really felt proud of myself. The time when I got to write the story title thing that went on the news.

Austin

Nerf Guns

I loved nerf guns. I used to shoot my brother and my mom. Nerf bullets bounced off the wall. I was crying. My brother held a nerf gun too and was shooting me. I was 5. He was seven and bigger. The nerf gun was green plastic. When I shot it, it went pfft.

Tennis

A moment I felt proud of myself was when I was playing tennis for the first time. I didn't know how to play because I was hitting the ball too hard, but I thought I was doing good, but my sister was saying no that's not how you play tennis. So I would always go to the park to practice. So I practiced for a month then when school started my teacher ask do you want to play tennis. So I said yeah. I remember my first match I won. I was proud of myself, but I spoke to myself and say I have to keep this momentum so all my matches I won then I had to face my biggest opponent for my tournament. I was just praying to god please let me win. And all I remember was me and my ponent was tie for game point, so I hit the ball really hard and fast to win and all I heard from the right was the ref said game and pointed at me. I was so proud of myself.

Roller Coaster

I remember I went to six flags and I seen a roller coaster. it look very fast and it was steep so I was telling my sister, "Let's go on it" and deep inside I was scared. So I remember me and my sister are sitting in the front so I got up and I took a deep breath. then the roller coaster start moving.

My Name

I remember when I was a baby I used to have a nickname. My family used to called me Jumbo. The reason why they call me Jumbo is because I used to eat a lot like I would eat everything when I was a baby. But I'd be so mad when my family use to call me Jumbo but I got used to it.

Ode to Bed

Risen from the debris of love
I stretch out in my big bed
silk sheet smooth
laid down hullabaloo, no frustration
3 small soft pillows
I feel relaxed and free
I think about my grandma
and God, memories I had
with her when she came and I hugged her tightly
When I fall asleep I don't have dreams
just dark
Banging or screaming wakes me up in the middle of the night
I play games on my phone and go back to sleep when I can

Eric

My Favorite Things

I saw my fav pants, hat, clothes, and my basketball court. My fav food seafood and my old earrings and I remember my old iPhone and I pictured my old blanket that I used when i was little. When I was playing basketball with my ball I won against my cousins and friends. My blanket was black, blue, red, and green and it glowed up in the dark. I used to use it all the time when I was a kid and i would take it when I go to my grandparents' house because it was comfortable.

Basketball

When me and my friend were playing basketball and I kept missing most of my shots. But when he started trash talking and I started to try hard to make every shot I put up and I won the game. Then we moved on to football and he did the same thing but I won and that's why you never trash talk and what trash talking does is make you mad and start a fight. But I still kept it cool.

My Name

I like my name because it is not too long. Only 4 letters. And imma jr and I glad I got a short name because I don't like long names so I'm glad with the name I got. And I like being a jr because it's cool and my middle name is Deonate and I got my middle name from my dad.

Community

My community is my family and it looks like they care for me. My mom cares for me and she's a part of my community and my community calls me out if I do something wrong, like my mom she'll call me out if I do something. She'll say what am I doing and stop doing what I'm doing.

My First Phone

The first time I got my phone I was happy and excited because that was my first time I had a phone. I could play my favorite games like Roblox, Minecraft, and Call of Duty. The next couple of months it dropped and broke and I gotta new phone and I did not drop it.

Gabriel (Middle School Teacher)

Gabriel (le)

When I was a baby, my mom and my grandmother gave me the name Gabrielle. My grandmother named all of my siblings: Anastasia, Anjelica, Jerrica, Stephan, and I think Javon. What's so special about my name is that it also chose me. Originally, I was set to be Gabrielle. When my mom was pregnant and giving birth, she was a little too medicated. She accidentally forgot to put the "LE". So birthed on August 18, 1997 Gabriel Rochell Clark was born. At first I hated my name. Everyone always expected a boy to walk in when they had Gabriel on their attendance sheet. I would always have to correct them by saying, "It's Gabrielle." Until one day I gave up on correcting people and went with the name the Universe gave me. So I confidently became Gabriel. Around 2012, I became Gabe! AI realized the name Gabriel/Gabe represented how unique and irreplaceable I was. In my mom's eyes I'll always be Gabrielle or Gabi...

Community

A community is a group of people who live together, love together, and grow together. In a community everyone plays a part and a place. In my community I am the lover and soul. My community is diverse. My community is special. My community is made up of biological and chosen family. My community is a community of believers. We believe in each other. We believe in dreams and goals. We push each other to grow. We hold each other accountable. We help each other when we can. We accept when we can't with love and understanding. We may not always be patient. Our community might have cracks and imperfections. We might argue and disagree but we are stuck like glue. My community trusts, loves, understands, persists, challenges.

MLK

My first time coming to MLK was intense. I came to work. I was nervous because I didn't know if the kids would like me. It almost felt like the first day of school in kindergarten. It was January, so I was more like a transfer kid that joined a new school in the middle of school. I had those feelings of they already know each other. I remember me wanting to build relationships but not wanting to be too pushy. I met all the staff before I met the kids. They were all so welcoming and kind. The kids were all so intrigued. They asked a bunch of questions. I found out that allowing them to ask about me help build our relationship. I first met the 4th and 5th grade group. They were welcoming but also wondering "who is this lady?" Towards the end of my day they warmed up and it felt like the start of something great. Now almost 7 months later we are cool as cucumbers. I love it here. And I think they love me here. Yay MLK!

Isaac

My First Time on a Plane

My first time on a plane was scary. I was afraid of heights. But when I looked outside it was beautiful. We flew over Hollywood and Las Vegas to get to Indy. Me and my brother were asleep and my mom was scared because the plane was shaking. We took three planes to get here. That's my first time on a plane.

I Am

I am ashes from a volcano.
I'm a young king that is waiting to rule.
I am a campfire that burns bright.
I'm someone's son, brother, cousin, uncle.
I'm meant to shine like everyone.
I'm sunshine to someone's rainy day.
I am a great grandchild.
I live to shine. I am a painter and the world is my canvas.
I'm a protestor. I have my rights.
I am an opera mask. I have different feelings.
I am a baseball player.
I swing at opportunities.
I am a generous that will soon come.
I am a writer. I put my thoughts into books.
I am a president. I think about my community first.
I stop war and give peace.
I am loved. I'm extraordinary. I'm great.

I am Mother Nature. I bring life to this world.
I am water. I flow through hard problems.
I am a paintbrush. I flow with the vibes.
I am wind the sky is not the limit.
I am a cloud. I soar over the bad situations.
I'm fire. I burn bright you need sunglasses to see me.
I'm water. I flow through problems.
I'm a dreamer. I go big.
I am greatness. I love food for someone's heart. I'm sunshine for someone's heart.
I am a companion. I stay by your side.
I'm space. I have endless possibilities.
I am a scholar. I move ahead.
I'm smart, kind.
I'm a mineral. I am rare.
I am chess. I'm a hard thinker.

What Makes Me Proud

What makes me proud of myself is my smartness and I can speak on all my thoughts. I can keep going and going about any subject and the greatness I bring to the world and country. I bring challenges that nobody can solve. What makes me proud of myself is my education and questions that I bring. And my kindness to others and compassion to others. Also my sportsmanship when we play games and sports. I love my thoughts when I'm into something like writing a story or a poem or when I can do things other people can't do. Also, my opportunities I have when I grow up.

Jai'Anna

Cousins

Ten cousins piled into the back of the truck. When we start moving, we start to sing "We Don't to go to Granny's house." We sing loud. My oldest cousin sings the loudest. We all start laughing but were still singing. We go around the block and then we stop and get out.

Myrtle Beach

When I was little, me and my family went to Myrtle Beach. We lived in one big house. It was a lot of us. My mom was pregnant with my sister. We played on the beach. We had fun at Myrtle beach!

My Name

I have many nicknames: JJ Money, JJ, Anna, Jai'anna, Senorita.
My uncle name me Jai'anna.
If I could have a different name I would be called Karmin.

My Community

My community is calm and we have a garden. We have a pool and a park. In my community everybody loves everybody.

James

Football

"I'm the best football player," said mo. "Can you prove it?" said Jaylen. "Bet let's start a game," said Mom. So we start the game but they made the rules and the rules are: Rule 1 Each point was worth 7. Rule 2 There are no blitz and no QB sneaks. Now they start the game and at first Jaylen's team was up by 7 points.

Jordyn

Pranks

I was in my brother's room with my little sister and my older sister and we were watching a movie with our brother. But, before all of this, my brother said whoever fell asleep first would have to get cold water poured on them. And unfortunately I fell asleep first and they poured a bucket of water on me while recording me and I almost drowned. Another time I laughed really hard was when me, my little sister, and older sister we went into our brother's room while he was downstairs and we stole his money and his hats and we tucked the money in our hats. But he ended up finding out that we had it.

My Name

My name was chosen by my parents because they wanted all my siblings to have J's, but one of my sister's names starts with an M. The nicknames my dad called me were Jorgie, Jar Jar, and Picklehead. Unfortunately I don't know if my mom gave me a nickname. My sisters' names are Jada, Journei, and then it's me Jordyn, and my little sister's name is Mikaylah. And I also have two brothers one of them passed when he was a baby and his name was little Nico, the same name after my dad. But my other brother's name is Jasper. If I could change my name I honestly think I wouldn't because it has a lot of strong memories behind it.

Kathy

Ode to Mom

If my mom was in danger
I would save her.

If my mom was a TV
I would watch her.

If my mom was paper
I would paint her.

I love my mom because she is the light of me. When I am hurt she heals. When I am down she gets me up. When I hurt she is there. She always made sure I was ok.

Me, Myself, and I

I come from majorettes. It has good dancers and big challenges, skill, and talent. I am from hair stylists. There's lots of combs and hair gel. People are there for a good 6-8 hours and they walk out cute with a good new hairstyle. I am from Roblox there is good games and voice chat to talk to people but be careful because they will ban you. I am from money there is green everywhere with numbers on them. People say money doesn't buy happiness but for me it does.

My Name

My name is Kathy. I was named after my auntie. My nickname is Goobee but I really don't like it. If I was to change it I would change it to Keke. Lots of people mess up my name when it's easy to say.

Community

I think it's a nice place where you can have peace. The people are nice and friendly and helpful.

They all come together and build a good community. Where it is judge free. We have dancers and pools. There's lots of people and my friends dance together.

Nikkal

Trash Talk

I was playing basketball with my black basketball outside in my driveway with my friends. We was playing 1 vs 1. There were spectators just sitting on the grass. When I hit a shot they yelled "Boom!" They yelled "boom" when my friend hit a shot, too. My body was moving. I dribbled and ran back and forth and shot the ball. It was hot. I was sweating. I was trash talking. My friend trash talked back. I won. My mom called me home for dinner.

Ode to My Game

I like my game because it is fun to play on like we can play GTA, Roblox, and Forza Horizons, Call of Duty and car games, and I like it because it is fun to play on. When I be playing it be fun to play because I be rating on the game I be having fun. I want to game

I Am From

I am from my home. My home is funny, interesting, and good. I am from a home with 7 people that are funny, interesting, loving, caring.

My Name

My name is always misspelled and said wrong. My nickname is JR, Baby K, K5. My name is Nikkail Merritt Jr. And my dad's name is Nikkail. I like to be named after my dad and they named me after my dad bc I act like him.

My Community

My community is a lot of people like Black people and white people. Lots of good people and bad people. My community is okay. Cars like hellcat SRT, Skat Pack, Kia.

Phillip

Ode to My Hoodie

My ode is to my hoodie.
My hoodie keeps me warm.
My hoodie walks me home.
It would be clean, warm, and comfortable
and spacious.

How To Be Me

I am from my Spotify playlist to my bed.
From my hoodie to my blanket.
To my toys, games and family.
I'm from my messed-up sleep schedule to my normal sleep.
I'm from my favorite food jambalaya to my most hated food fish.
I'm from my Xbox to my controller.
From my bad handwriting to my good math problem solving.
From the end zone to the football.
I'm from my free time to my busiest time of the day.

My Name

I got my name from my mom and dad. My parents were going to name me Phillip. I like my name because it is easy to say and spell. My aunt calls me PJ or JR. When my cousin comes over, his name is Phillip too, so we call him Phillip and call me Phill Phill.

If I had a different name it would be Phillip with an F spelled Fillip. I feel connected to my dad cause I have the same name as him. If I really had to change my name I would change it to Shanks. I would not have any nick names.

My Idea of a Community

The community is my family I see every day at home. The community I wanna make is a one with less violence. With less theft. The people in my community most are smart, strong people. But most of them are not good people. The things I see people doing drinking, vaping, stealing, hurting each other. Some of them are good and that's enough.

My First Phone

I got my first phone. I asked for a chocolate bar and I got a phone. He left and I waited. It felt like a long time for a nine-year-old. I sat and waited and waited and my dad came back with a phone and I was mad cause I didn't get a bar it was just a phone bar. My dad got told by my mom to get me a phone instead.

Sirion

Trains and Cars

My mom and dad got me Thomas trains for my first birthday. I played all day. I had red and silver cars. I played in the bathroom and the silver one got stuck behind the toilet. I couldn't reach it and I didn't like to ask for help, so I left it there. I didn't feel bad because I had a bigger one.

Syncere

My Little Shirt

I saw my old Mickey Mouse shirt out the corner of my eye. It was black and white with a slash of orange and green in certain spots. I started to remember that I wore this shirt everywhere. My favorite time to wear it was when we went out to eat. Every time we went out to eat I always got compliments about it and they made my little heart patter. I was so upset and heartbroken when I could not fit in it anymore, so I cut and stitched it so it would fit the dog so I still got to see my favorite shirt every day

I Am from FRENZY

I am from a dark corner filled with luminous light that shines bright above me.
I am from a future that is wealthy and famous.
I am from high expectations meaning I have to have high goals.
I am from a strong mindset and point of view.
I am from a very heavy bundle of emotions and opinions.
Nobody has to agree with me that's what makes every quaking bone in my body different.
That's what makes me me.

The Camping Trip

I woke up to my lovely mother's beautiful and angelic voice saying we are going camping. I sprung out of bed and screamed "YAY!" As I was jumping on the bed eeek errrn CRASH. The bed fell through the bed spring. My mother's smile faded as fast as a blink of the eye. "NOW I HAVE TO REPLACE THE BED I JUST BOUGHT!!" After she scolded me for about 12 minutes, we went and had breakfast at Denny's. As they were bringing us our food they gave us the wrong order and when we ask them to fix it or reimburse us they refused. We left with huge attitudes. When we got to the campgrounds they were gorgeous. They reminded me of how beautiful nature could be so all of my trouble blew away with the wind.

Ode to Friends

This is an ode to my very best friends Ryann and Rayla. They are always there and they make me feel loved and appreciated. They are the only people in my life who don't make fun of me for my music taste. They learned to enjoy and embrace K-pop and the Korean culture for me.

They don't try to point out our differences, but they make sure to point out our similarities. Even though I tend to annoy them (sometimes on purpose) they love me unconditionally. I love them just as much and I hope they trust and believe in me as much as I trust and believe in them.

Quote: Things are never quite scary when you have your best friend. – Bill Watterson

My Mom's Beautiful Brown Eyes

My mom, Brittany Levi, is a colossal part of my life. She is an amazing person filled with life and joy. She has a beautiful golden-brown buzz cut with gorgeous brown eyes. She makes my whole world turn. We chortle together, we cry together. When I need her she's there.

Even though I constantly get on her nerves, she continues to love me anyways. "From the moon and back and through thick and thin". To me those are more than words. Those are a gateway to happiness. And when things get hard we'll pick each other up. She helps me comb my hair and put on bow ties. That is why I love her beautiful brown eyes.

The Origin

My name is Syncere Lee Parker-Hershey. It is unique yet very common. It stands for smart, youthful, nourishing, capable, energetic, radiant, and elegant. These words represent everything I stand for and that's why I love it. I don't know who gave me my first name and honestly I don't want to know (mysterious). I got my middle name from my favorite uncle David Lee Brown. I got my last name from my dad, James Parker-Hershey. It all came together super well. No other name would fit my brand and the way I casually live my life. My name to me means respect and give and you get two streets exist for a reason. I also own a unique nickname Sy (pronounced Sai). My name is mine and I wouldn't trade it for the world.

Writing Prompts

Below are the prompts used to trigger students' memories and help them decide on a story they wanted to tell. We encourage you to try them yourselves!

- Tell me story about a time when you felt tough and brave.
- Tell the story about what happened when something made you laugh so hard your stomach hurt—or worse!
- Tell the story about what happened when someone played a trick on you or embarrassed you in some way. Or tell the story of what happened when you played a trick on or embarrassed someone else.
- Tell the story about what happened the first time you…. (whatever).
- Imagine your best day ever. What would you do? Where would you go? Who would be with you?
- Write an ode to something or someone you love. (Inspired by Kwame Alexander's "Ode to My Hair")
- Tell the story of where you come from (Inspired by George Ella Lyon's "I Come From")
- Since you asked, I'll tell you why I'm _____ (angry, worried, scared, in love, sad, hopeless, fearful, etc.…)
- Tell the story about what happened something went differently than you expected it to go.
- Tell the story of your name. Are you named after anyone? Do you have a nickname? How did you get your nickname? How do you feel about your name?

- Tell the story about what happened when you met someone important to you.
- Tell the story about what happened when you were really proud of yourself.
- Dr. Martin Luther King Jr spoke of a "beloved community". Who is in your beloved community? Where are your favorite places to go in your beloved community? What would you like to change about your community?
- Write a letter to your future self. Do you have any regrets to apologize for? What are the dreams and goals that you're most excited about? What advice do you have for yourself? What questions do you have for your future self?

www.ingramcontent.com/pod-product-compliance
Lightning Source LLC
Chambersburg PA
CBHW052148070526
44585CB00017B/2031